Horses & Painted Moments

ADULT COLORING BOOK WITH POETRY AND SELF-DISCOVERY

Aventuras De Viaje

Copyright SF Nonfiction Books © 2024

All Rights Reserved

No part of this document may be reproduced without written consent from the author.

www.SFNonfictionBooks.com

INTRODUCTION

Welcome to a captivating world where the grace of horses converges with the realm of creativity, where the timeless allure of these majestic creatures meets the strokes of imagination. This is not merely a coloring book—it's a journey, a reflection, and a celebration of the inspiring beauty of horses and the painted moments they inspire.

Each page invites you to explore a realm filled with detailed illustrations of various horse breeds and scenes, from the noble Arabian to other majestic horses, all awaiting your colors to bring them to life. These scenes, symbols of the world's rich equestrian heritage, call for your colors to reveal their stories. Coloring these moments offers not only a visual journey but also a profound connection with the majestic wonders of the equine world.

In the hustle of our daily lives, finding moments to pause and appreciate the wonders of nature is invaluable. This book encourages you to slow down, immerse yourself in a world of intricate artistry and serene introspection, and reconnect with the timeless elegance of horses and creativity. It's an opportunity to reignite your imagination and infuse it with the colors of grace and self-discovery.

Begin this artistic journey, exploring the detailed realm of horses and the calming act of coloring. Here, you're not just witnessing the beauty of these magnificent animals; you're engaging with their wonders, unleashing your creativity, and experiencing the tranquility of artistic mindfulness.

Discovering the Mosaic of Imagination

Dive deeper, and you'll find that this book has been meticulously crafted to enhance your personal journey:

- **Simple Activities:** Beyond just coloring, engage with activities designed to spark reflection and creativity. These gentle prompts will lead you to moments of introspection, serving as kindling for your inner fire.

- **Quotes:** Let the wisdom of personal development accompany you, illuminating your path as you add your own burst of color to the pages.

- **Positive Affirmations:** As you color, let these words of positivity uplift your spirit, molding your thoughts and inspiring a brighter perspective.

- **Poems and Haikus**: Delight in the poetic tales that complement the theme of this book, capturing life's varied rhythms and experiences. Each verse and every line serve as a muse for your artistic endeavors, enhancing your coloring journey with lyrical inspiration.

Embark on this coloring odyssey, immersing yourself in a world of diverse themes and the therapeutic embrace of art. Each page invites you on a unique journey, blending your creativity with the tranquility of coloring.

THANKS FOR YOUR PURCHASE

Get Your Next SF Nonfiction Book FREE!

Claim the book of your choice at:

www.SFNonfictionBooks.com/Free-Book

You will also be among the first to know of all the latest releases, discount offers, bonus content, and more.

Go to:

www.SFNonfictionBooks.com/Free-Book

Thanks again for your support.

Morning Ride:
Describe a moment of peace you experienced recently.

_____

_____

"The way to overcome obstacles is like riding a horse; just keep moving forward with grace and determination."

I embrace the strength and grace of a horse within me.

In fields of green,
horses roam free,
their spirit wild,
just like the sea.

**Galloping Dreams:
Write about a dream or goal that inspires you.**

_____

_____

"Like a horse, embrace the wildness within you to discover your true strength."

I am as free as a wild horse, untamed and full of spirit.

Galloping through fields,
Manes flowing in the soft breeze,
Nature's pure embrace.

Equine Elegance:
Share a compliment you received
or gave that brightened your day.

_____

_____

"In the rhythm of the hoofbeats, find the courage to face your fears."

I am connected to the natural world and its beauty.

Beneath the sky,
so vast and bright,
horses run with all their might.

Trailblazing Moments:
Describe a time when you felt truly free.

_____

_____

"Grace and power come from knowing when to gallop and when to rest."

I embrace my inner wildness and let it guide me.

Hooves echo softly,
Whispers in the morning light,
Peaceful harmony.

Hoofbeats of Happiness:
Share something that made you laugh this week.

_____

_____

"Feel the wind of change like a horse running through an open field."

I trust in my ability to navigate life's challenges.

Through valleys deep and mountains high,
horses journey, reaching the sky.

Mane Moments:
Reflect on a small act of kindness you witnessed or performed.

_____

_____

"Harness the power within you, as a horse harnesses its strength in every stride."

I am graceful in my movements and actions.

Strong and fierce they stand,
Graceful strides across the land,
Freedom in their hearts.

Grazing Gratitude:
Reflect on a meal or food you enjoyed and why it made you happy.

_____

_____

"In the eyes of a horse, see the reflection of your own potential."

I am open to new adventures and experiences.

In twilight's glow, they gently tread, where dreams and reality are softly spread.

Wild Wonder:
Reflect on a time when you felt awe or wonder in nature.

_____

_____

"In every gallop, there's a lesson in perseverance and resilience."

I am loyal and trustworthy, like a faithful horse.

Silent in the night,
Horses move with quiet grace,
Moonlight guides their way.

**Sunset Silhouette:
Describe a beautiful scene you witnessed recently.**

_____

_____

"In the wild freedom of nature,
find your own liberation."

I am in tune with my inner strength and wisdom.

With manes that dance in the wind's embrace, horses teach us strength and grace.

Harmony in the Herd:
Write about a time you felt connected with others.

_____

_____

"In every stride, there is a lesson; in every stumble, there is a new strength."

I am at peace with who I am.

Fields of endless green,
Horses run with spirits high,
Nature's serene scene.

**Hoofbeats of Hope:
Reflect on something that gives you hope.**

_____

_____

"Embrace change with the same enthusiasm as running through a new pasture."

I am calm and centered, like a horse in a quiet stable.

In morning mist, their shapes appear,
horses bring us hope and cheer.

**Courageous Canter:
Reflect on a challenge you overcame.**

_____

_____

"The journey of self-discovery is much like a long journey: full of ups and downs, but always forward."

I am free to express my true self.

Morning dew on grass,
Horses graze as dawn breaks clear,
Life's new day begins.

Foal's First Steps:
Describe a new skill or hobby you've started.

_____

_____

"Patience in training teaches us the value of persistence in personal growth."

BEYOND THESE PAGES

A Deeper Dive into Art and Soul Awaits!

This book is but a chapter in a voyage where creativity meets depth.

Craving more? Explore the link below and weave deeper into the tapestry of art and emotion.

www.SFNonfictionBooks.com/Adult-Coloring-Books

A HEARTFELT THANK YOU

Dear colorist,

Thank you for choosing this book. If you enjoyed your journey, please leave a review where you purchased it. Your feedback helps more than you might think.

As the colors on these pages come to life, so does our shared journey in this artistic realm. I am deeply grateful for your trust and for allowing this book to be part of your self-care and personal journey.

By coloring these pages, you've not just created art but also woven moments of peace, reflection, and creativity into your life.

If you wish to explore more, there are other themes awaiting your artistic touch. Dive into new worlds and let your imagination flow.

From the deepest corner of my heart, thank you for bringing this book to life. Until our next artistic adventure together, cherish the colors of your journey and continue to shine.

Warmly,

Aventuras De Viaje

ABOUT THE AUTHOR

Aventuras has three passions: travel, writing, and learning new skills.

Combining these three things, Miss Viaje spends her time exploring the world and learning about anything and everything that interests her, from yoga, to music, to science, and more.

Aventuras takes what she discovers and shares it through her books.

www.SFNonfictionBooks.com

www.ingramcontent.com/pod-product-compliance
Lightning Source LLC
Chambersburg PA
CBHW081621100526
44590CB00021B/3542